Ice Cream Dream

by Lynn Trepicchio
illustrations by Jackie Snider

H a r c o u r t   B r a c e   &   C o m p a n y

Orlando Atlanta Austin Boston San Francisco Chicago Dallas New York Toronto London

An Ice Cream Dream
is a treat to eat.

2

How do you make an
Ice Cream Dream?
I'll teach you.

You need at least three friends—three friends who like a real treat—three friends who like to eat.

Get a big, deep dish.
Heap lots of ice cream
into the dish. Heap on
lots of treats.

Put on whipped cream.
Give a cheer! Take a
seat and say "Please."

With speed, reach for your
Ice Cream Dream.
What a feast to eat!
What a treat!

Why is it an Ice Cream
Dream? After it has been
eaten, when the plates are
all clean—sweet dreams!